EDUCATION IN A COMPETITIVE AND GLOBALIZING WORLD

AN ENQUIRY INTO SARVA SHIKSHA ABHIYAN: THE UNIVERSAL ELEMENTARY EDUCATION PROGRAMME OF INDIA

EDUCATION IN A COMPETITIVE AND GLOBALIZING WORLD

Additional books in this series can be found on Nova's website under the Series tab.

Additional E-books in this series can be found on Nova's website under the E-books tab.

EDUCATION IN A COMPETITIVE AND GLOBALIZING WORLD

AN ENQUIRY INTO SARVA SHIKSHA ABHIYAN: THE UNIVERSAL ELEMENTARY EDUCATION PROGRAMME OF INDIA

DIGANTA MUKHERJEE

Nova Science Publishers, Inc.
New York

Copyright © 2011 by Nova Science Publishers, Inc.

All rights reserved. No part of this book may be reproduced, stored in a retrieval system or transmitted in any form or by any means: electronic, electrostatic, magnetic, tape, mechanical photocopying, recording or otherwise without the written permission of the Publisher.

For permission to use material from this book please contact us:
Telephone 631-231-7269; Fax 631-231-8175
Web Site: http://www.novapublishers.com

NOTICE TO THE READER

The Publisher has taken reasonable care in the preparation of this book, but makes no expressed or implied warranty of any kind and assumes no responsibility for any errors or omissions. No liability is assumed for incidental or consequential damages in connection with or arising out of information contained in this book. The Publisher shall not be liable for any special, consequential, or exemplary damages resulting, in whole or in part, from the readers' use of, or reliance upon, this material.

Independent verification should be sought for any data, advice or recommendations contained in this book. In addition, no responsibility is assumed by the publisher for any injury and/or damage to persons or property arising from any methods, products, instructions, ideas or otherwise contained in this publication.

This publication is designed to provide accurate and authoritative information with regard to the subject matter covered herein. It is sold with the clear understanding that the Publisher is not engaged in rendering legal or any other professional services. If legal or any other expert assistance is required, the services of a competent person should be sought. FROM A DECLARATION OF PARTICIPANTS JOINTLY ADOPTED BY A COMMITTEE OF THE AMERICAN BAR ASSOCIATION AND A COMMITTEE OF PUBLISHERS.

Additional color graphics may be available in the e-book version of this book.

LIBRARY OF CONGRESS CATALOGING-IN-PUBLICATION DATA

Mukherjee, Diganta.
 An enquiry into Sarva Shiksha Abhiyan : the universial elementary education programme of india / Diganta Mukherjee.
   p. cm. -- (Education in a competitive and globalizing world)
 Includes bibliographical references and index.
 ISBN 978-1-61122-976-9 (softcover : alk. paper)
 1. Sarva Shiksha Abhiyan (Program) 2. Education, Elementary--Standards--India 3. Education, Preschool--Standards--India 4. Educational equalization--India. I. Title.
 LA1152.M8498 2011
 372'.954--dc22
                    2010046842

Published by Nova Science Publishers, Inc. ✢ *New York*

Contents

Preface		vii
Chapter 1	Introduction	1
Chapter 2	Sarva Shiksha Abhiyan	3
Chapter 3	The Scenario of West Bengal	27
Chapter 4	Results of the Primary Field Survey	31
Chapter 5	Qualitative Analysis	41
Chapter 6	Recommendations	45
References		53
Index		55

Preface

It is an established fact that basic education improves the level of human well-being especially with regard to life expectancy, infant mortality and nutritional status of children, as well as a significant contribution to economic growth. Universal Elementary Education (UEE) has arranged a programme called "Sarba Shiksha Abhiyan". It is a historic stride towards achieving the long cherished goal of Universalisation of Elementary Education (UEE) through a time bound integrated approach, in partnership with States. This book provides an in depth examination of the educational program called "Sarba Shiksha Abhiyan".

Chapter 1

INTRODUCTION

Social justice and equity are by themselves a strong argument for providing basic education for all. Every child has a right for quality education. It is an established fact that basic education improves the level of human well-being especially with regard to life expectancy, infant mortality, nutritional status of children, etc as well as it significantly contributes to economic growth too.

Universal Elementary Education (UEE) has arranged a programme called "Sarba Shiksha Abhiyan". It is a historic stride towards achieving the long cherished goal of Universalisation of Elementary Education (UEE) through a time bound integrated approach, in partnership with States. SSA, which promises to change the face of the elementary education sector of the country, aims to provide useful and quality elementary education to all children in the 6-14 age groups by 2010. Adequate, rigorous, inclusive and continuous monitoring and supervision are one of the most important keys to successful implementation of any educational programme.

For success of any programme, the most important aspect is the proper formation of the strategy and its successful implementation. Without proper framework or structure Sarva Shiksha Abhiyan, flagship programme of Government of India (GOI), would not be successful. In this project, we have tried to study the existing framework of Sarva Siksha Abhiyan with the help of primary and secondary data. To collect primary data, 9 schools have been surveyed mainly from North and Central Kolkata. In each school, we have interviewed 10 students and 2 teachers. All details are given in the field survey part.

Chapter 2

SARVA SHIKSHA ABHIYAN

Sarva Shiksha Abhiyan (SSA) is the Government of India's (GoI) flagship programme launched in 2001 to achieve the goal of Universalization of Elementary Education. The major goals of the programme are:

- All children in school by 2005.
- Focus on satisfactory quality with emphasis on education for life
- Bridging gender and social gaps in primary by 2007 and in elementary by 2010
- Universal retention by 2010

The Mission's approach is one of learning - to understand the progress made under the programme and to indicate experiences that highlight strengths and weaknesses, with a view to strengthening implementation. The Mission has reviewed progress towards the programme goals. This review is based on our study of available documents and discussions with national and state level functionaries.

Sarva Shiksha Abhiyan has proven to be one the of most successful missions launched by the Government of India with whole-hearted participation of states which is increasingly deepening down to the village-habitation, and school level. It is also a program that holds tremendous promise considering the best practices and energy it continues to generate.

Sarva Shiksha Abhiyan (SSA) has evolved from the recommendation of the state education ministers' conference held in October 1998 that universal elementary education should be pursued in mission mode. A national committee of state education ministers under the chairmanship of the minister for HRD was set up on the recommendation of the conference to work out the approach. It submitted its report in October 1999. The scheme was approved by the Union Cabinet in its meeting held on 16 November 2000 and became functional from January 2001. SSA is a programme to provide useful and relevant elementary education for all children in the age group of 6 to 14 years by 2010, with the active participation of the community by effectively involving the panchayat institutions, school management committees, village and urban slum level education committees, parent teacher associations, mother-teacher associations, tribal autonomous councils and other grass root level structures in the management of schools to bridge social, regional and gender gaps. The programme realized the importance of early childhood care and education and looked at the 0-14 age as a continuum and had the following important objectives:

- to have all children in school, education guarantee centre(EGC), alternate school(ASC), and back to school (BSC) camp by 2003, Since revised to 2005, in March 2005
- to ensure that all children complete five years of primary schooling by 2007.
- to ensure that all children complete eight years of elementary schooling by 2010.
- focus on elementary education of satisfactory quality with emphasis on education for life.
- bridge all gender and social category gaps at the primary stage by 2007 and at the elementary education level by 2010 and
- achieve universal retention by 2010.

2.1. SCOPE OF THE PROGRAMME

The initiatives under SSA have broadly been grouped under the following heads:

- Preparatory activities for micro-planning, household surveys, studies, community mobilization, school–based activities, training and orientation at all levels,
- Appointment of teachers,
- Opening new primary and alternative schooling facilities like Education Guarantee Scheme (EGS)/Alternative and Innovative Education centers (AIE),

- Opening of upper primary schools,
- Construction of additional classrooms, schools and other facilities,
- Provision of free textbooks to all girls and SC/ST children,
- Maintenance and repair of school buildings,
- Provision of teaching/learning equipment for primary schools on up gradation of EGS to regular schools or setting up of a new primary school,
- TLE for upper primary school,
- School grant,
- Teacher grant,
- Teacher training,
- Opening of State Institute of Educational Management and Training (SIEMAT),
- Training of community leaders,
- Provision for disabled children,
- Research, Evaluation, Supervision and Monitoring,
- Management cost,
- Innovative activity for girls' education, early childhood care and education, interventions for children belonging to SC/ST community, computer education specially for upper primary level,
- Setting up Block Resource Centre (BRC)/Cluster Resource Centre (CRC), and
- Interventions for out of school children.

2.2. NORMS FOR INTERVENTIONS UNDER SSA

INTERVENTION	NORM
Teacher	One teacher for every 40 children in Primary and Upper primary schools. At least two teachers in a Primary school
School/Alternative schooling facility	Within one Kilometer of every habitation
Upper Primary schools / Sector	As per requirement based on the number of children completing primary education, up to a ceiling of one upper primary school / section for every two primary schools
Class Rooms	A room for every teacher in Primary and upper primary A room for Head Master in upper Primary school /sector
Free textbooks	To all girls/SC/ST children at primary and upper primary level within an upper ceiling of Rs.150/- per child
Civil works	Ceiling of 33% of SSA programme funds. For improvements of school facilities, BRC/CRC construction. No expenditure to be incurred on construction of office buildings
Maintenance and repair of school buildings	Only through school management committees Upto Rs. 5000 per year as per a specific proposal by the school committee. Must involve elements of community contribution
Upgradation of EGS to regular school	Provision of TLE @ Rs 10, 000/- per school Provision for teacher and classrooms
TLE for upper primary	@ Rs 50,000 per school for uncovered schools
Schools grant	Rs. 2000/- per year per primary / upper primary school for replacement of school equipments
Teacher grant	Rs 500 per teacher per year in primary and upper primary
Teacher training	Provision of 20 days in service for all teachers, 60 days refresher courses for untrained teacher and 30 day orientation for freshly trained recruits @ Rs.70/- per day
State Institute of Educational Management Administration and Training (SIEMAT)	One time assistance up to Rs.3 Crore
Training of community leaders	For a maximum of 8 persons in a village for 2 days @ Rs. 30/- per day
Provision for disabled children	Upto Rs. 1500 per school per year By creating pool of resource persons, providing travel grant and honorarium for monitoring generation of community based data, research studies, cost of assessment and appraisal terms and their field activities

NORMS FOR INTERVENTIONS UNDER SSA (CONTINUED)

Management Cost	Not to exceed 6% of the budget of a district plan
Innovative activity for girls education, early childhood care and education, interventions for children belonging to SC/ST community, computer education specially for upper primary level	Upto to Rs. 15 lakhs for each innovative project and Rs. 50 lakhs for a district will apply for SSA
Block Resource Centers / Cluster / Resource Centers	Rs. 6 lakh ceiling for BRC construction wherever required Rs. 2 lakh for CRC construction wherever required Deployment of up to 20 teacher in a block with more their 100 schools Provision of furniture etc. @ Rs. 1 lakh for a BRC and Rs. 10,000 for a CRC Contingency grant of Rs. 12,500 for a BRC and Rs. 2500 per CRC, per year
Interventions for out of school children	As per norms already approved under Education Guarantee Scheme and Alternative and Innovative Education, providing for the following kind of interventions. Setting up Education Guarantee Centers in unserved habitations Setting other alternative schooling models Bridge Courses, remedial courses, Back to School Camps with a focus on mainstreaming out of school children into regular schools.
Preparatory activities for Micro planning, household surveys, studies, community mobilization, school based activities, office equipments, etc.	As per specific proposal

Source: Ministry of Human Resource Development.

2.3. EXISTING MANAGEMENT STRUCTURE

The Prime Minister is the Chairman of the General Council of Sarva Shiksha Abhiyan National Mission. National Mission comprises the General Council, which is headed by the Prime Minister, and the Minister of Human Resource Development as shown in the Organogram heads the Executive Committee. The Minister for Human Resource Development is the Chairman and the Secretary, Department of Elementary Education, the Vice Chairman of the Executive Committee. A Bureau of Elementary Education headed by a Joint Secretary who is assisted by five Deputy Secretaries/ Directors as Divisional Heads has been constituted for overseeing implementation of the scheme. An Implementation Society (SIS) has been established in every State under the chairmanship of the Chief Minister/ Education Minister of the State/UT. The District Collector/ Magistrate/ Chief Executive Officer of the Zila Parishad oversees the district level implementation. The District Elementary Education Officer oversees the implementation of the programme at the district level. The organogram depicting the organizational set-up of SSA is given below:

2.3.1. Management Structure at the National Level

One of the basic features of the Sarva Shiksha Abhiyan is that the mainstream structures will primarily be used for implementing the programme. A separate Department of Elementary Education and Literacy has already been created for this purpose. In order to facilitate convergence and a holistic perspective, a single Bureau of Elementary Education has been constituted. The General Council at the National level will be headed by the Hon'ble Prime Minister with the Human Resource Development Minister as the Vice-Chairman. The Chairman of the Executive Committee will be the Hon'ble Human Resource Development Minister. The Secretary, Department of Elementary Education and Literacy will be the Vice-Chairperson of the Executive Committee. The Joint Secretary (Elementary Education) will also be the Director General of the National Mission of Sarva Shiksha Mission. He/she shall be the Member Secretary of the General Council and the Executive Committee. The Directors/ Deputy Secretaries of the National Mission will also work as the Deputy Director Generals of the National Mission under the overall supervision of the DG. Each DS/Director shall have specific functional and geographic responsibility.

2.3.2. Organisational Set Up at State Level

As per the framework drawn for implementation of SSA Programme, there would be a State Mission Authority for Universal Elementary Education (UEE). The States have to set up the "State Level Implementation Society (SIS)". In DPEP States, the existing Societies suitably modified would meet the needs of UEE.

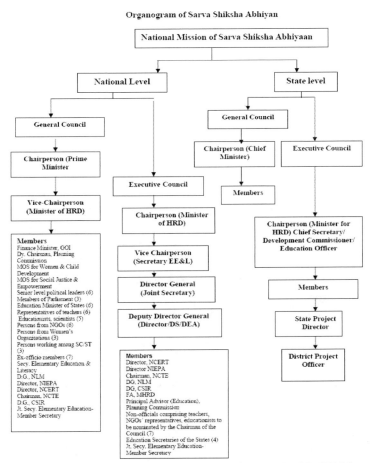

Source: Ministry of Human Resource Department (Report No. 15 of 2006).

Figure 1.

The SIS will carry out monitoring and operational support tasks. The District and Sub-district units will be set up by the state. The West Bengal Government, established on 2nd February 1995, a registered society named "Paschim Banga Rajya Prathamik Siksha Unnayan Sansita" as an autonomous and independent body for implementation of the West Bengal Elementary Education Project and to function as a societal mission for bringing about a fundamental change in the basic education system. The implementation of SSA in the WB State was entrusted to this State Mission on 14th March 2002 with some alterations. The name of SIS was also changed as "Paschim Banga Rajya Praramvik Siksha Unnayan Sanstha". The authorities of the Society are the General Council (GC) and the Executive Committee (EC). The GC is headed by the Chief Minister, with MIC, School Education as working President and MOS, School Education as Vice-president. The EC, which administers the affairs of the Society, is chaired by the Secretary to Government, School Education Department. The State Project Office is the most crucial unit for implementation of the programme, which has links with District and sub-district level structures, NGOs, State Govt., National Bureau and all other concerned. The Dist. Level Implementation Authority is headed by the Dist. Collector, which implements and reviews the progress of the Programme. After the district level, there are Block Level Structures to provide academic support and supervision, monitor implementation at grass root level and act as a vital link between the field and the District Projects Office. At the bottom, the Village Education Committee (VEC) prepares the plan for local needs and monitors school level interventions and works towards community ownership of the school.

The organizational chart (visual representation) depicting the flow of authority from the State Mission to School Level for successful implementation of the Scheme is indicated below:

(A) General Council

As per Rule 15 of the Memorandum of Association (MoA) of the SIS, the General Council shall meet at least twice in a year. Against this the G.C. met only once during 2002-03 (20.01.04) and 2003-04 (19.04.05).

(B) Executive Committee

Rule 32 of the MoA of the SIS stipulates that the Executive Committee shall meet at least once in every quarter of the year. Against this, the Executive Committee met only once each in 2002-03 (08.05.02), 2003- 04 (20.10.03) and 2004-05 (03.01.05).

(C) District Level Implementation Authority (DLIA)

The DLIA shall meet once in a month, and this should have met 24 times during 2003-04 and 2004-05. But from records it is seen that DLIA had met only thrice in 2003-04 and seven times in 2004-05.

(D) Block Level Structure

No data was made available to the Study Team regarding status of Block Level Structure.

ORGANISATIONAL CHART

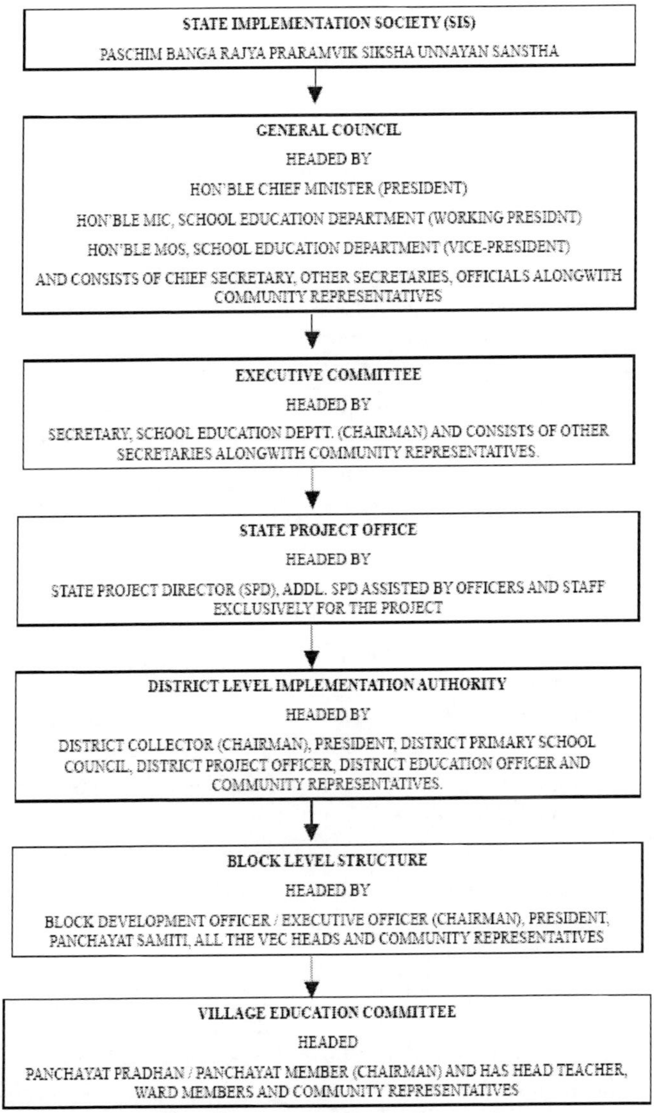

```
┌─────────────────────────────────────────────────────────────┐
│              STATE IMPLEMENTATION SOCIETY (SIS)              │
│    PASCHIM BANGA RAJYA PRARAMVIK SIKSHA UNNAYAN SANSTHA      │
└─────────────────────────────────────────────────────────────┘
                              ↓
┌─────────────────────────────────────────────────────────────┐
│                      GENERAL COUNCIL                         │
│                         HEADED BY                            │
│              HON'BLE CHIEF MINISTER (PRESIDENT)              │
│    HON'BLE MIC, SCHOOL EDUCATION DEPARTMENT (WORKING PRESIDNT)│
│    HON'BLE MOS, SCHOOL EDUCATION DEPARTMENT (VICE-PRESIDENT) │
│  AND CONSISTS OF CHIEF SECRETARY, OTHER SECRETARIES, OFFICIALS│
│            ALONGWITH COMMUNITY REPRESENTATIVES               │
└─────────────────────────────────────────────────────────────┘
                              ↓
┌─────────────────────────────────────────────────────────────┐
│                     EXECUTIVE COMMITTEE                      │
│                         HEADED BY                            │
│  SECRETARY, SCHOOL EDUCATION DEPTT. (CHAIRMAN) AND CONSISTS  │
│  OF OTHER SECRETARIES ALONGWITH COMMUNITY REPRESENTATIVES.   │
└─────────────────────────────────────────────────────────────┘
                              ↓
┌─────────────────────────────────────────────────────────────┐
│                     STATE PROJECT OFFICE                     │
│                         HEADED BY                            │
│  STATE PROJECT DIRECTOR (SPD), ADDL. SPD ASSISTED BY OFFICERS│
│           AND STAFF EXCLUSIVELY FOR THE PROJECT              │
└─────────────────────────────────────────────────────────────┘
                              ↓
┌─────────────────────────────────────────────────────────────┐
│              DISTRICT LEVEL IMPLEMENTATION AUTHORITY         │
│                         HEADED BY                            │
│   DISTRICT COLLECTOR (CHAIRMAN), PRESIDENT, DISTRICT PRIMARY │
│   SCHOOL COUNCIL, DISTRICT PROJECT OFFICER, DISTRICT         │
│   EDUCATION OFFICER AND COMMUNITY REPRESENTATIVES.           │
└─────────────────────────────────────────────────────────────┘
                              ↓
┌─────────────────────────────────────────────────────────────┐
│                     BLOCK LEVEL STRUCTURE                    │
│                         HEADED BY                            │
│   BLOCK DEVELOPMENT OFFICER / EXECUTIVE OFFICER (CHAIRMAN),  │
│   PRESIDENT, PANCHAYAT SAMITI, ALL THE VEC HEADS AND         │
│              COMMUNITY REPRESENTATIVES                       │
└─────────────────────────────────────────────────────────────┘
                              ↓
┌─────────────────────────────────────────────────────────────┐
│                   VILLAGE EDUCATION COMMITTEE                │
│                           HEADED                             │
│  PANCHAYAT PRADHAN / PANCHAYAT MEMBER (CHAIRMAN) AND HAS     │
│  HEAD TEACHER, WARD MEMBERS AND COMMUNITY REPRESENTATIVES    │
└─────────────────────────────────────────────────────────────┘
```

Source: Study on monitoring the financial aspects relating to Sarva Siksha Abhiyan in West Bengal sponsored by Ministry of Human Resource Department.

Figure 2.

2.4. FINANCE

According to broad assessments made by the Department of Elementary Education and Literacy, nearly Rs. 60,000 crore additional resources are required from the budget of the Central and the State level Departments over the next ten years. Since SSA is a programme for universalization of elementary education, the actual requirements of funds can only be worked out after the District Elementary Education Plans are finalized. Sarva Shiksha Abhiyan (SSA) has two aspects – I) It provides a wide convergent framework for implementation of Elementary Education schemes; II) It is also a programme with budget provision for strengthening vital areas to achieve universalization of elementary education. While all investments in the elementary education sector from the State and the Central Plans will reflect as part of the SSA framework, they will all merge into the SSA programme within the next few years. As a programme, it reflects the additional resource provision for UEE.

2.4.1. Financial Norms

- The assistance under the programme of Sarva Shiksha Abhiyan could be on an 85:15 sharing arrangement during the IX Plan, 72:24 sharing arrangement during the X Plan, and 50:50 thereafter between the Central government and State governments. Commitments regarding sharing of costs would be taken from State governments in writing.
- State will be required to maintain their level of allocation for elementary education in real terms on the base year 1999-2000. The share of states under SSA programme will be over and above the base year allocation.
- The Government of India would release funds to the State Governments/ Union Territories only and installments (except first) would only be released after the previous installments of Central government and State share has been transferred to the state Implementation Society.
- The support for teacher salary appointed under the SSA programme could be shared between the central government and the State government in a ratio of 85:15 during the IX Plan, 75:25 during the X plan and 50:50 thereafter.

- All legal agreements regarding externally assisted projects will continue to apply unless specific modifications have been agreed to, in consultation with foreign funding agencies.
- Existing schemes of elementary education of the Department (except National Bal Bhawan and NCTE) will converge after the IX Plan. The National Programme for Nutritional Support to Primary Education (Mid Day Meal) would remain a district intervention with food grains and specified transportation costs being met by the Centre and the cost of cooked meals being met by the State Government.
- District Education Plans would inter-alia; clearly show the funds/resource available for various components under schemes like JRY, PMRY, Sunishchit Rozgar Yojana, Area fund of MPs/MLAs, State Plan, Foreign Funding and resource generated in the NGO sector.
- All funds to be used for upgradation, maintenance, repair of schools and Teaching Learning Equipment and local management to be transferred to VECs/ School Management Committees.
- Other incentive schemes like distribution of scholarships and uniforms will continue to be funded under the State Plan. They will not be funded the SSA programme.

2.4.2 Funding Pattern

The expenditure under SSA was financed during the IX Five Year Plan on 85:15 basis by Union and State Governments. The ratio was changed to 75:25 during X Plan and 50:50 thereafter. Union Government's share was partly (30 *per cent*) financed by the external agencies in the shape of soft loan and grant. The following chart would show financing pattern for the period 2003-2007:

External financing comprised funds received from:

1) World Bank's International Development Association (IDA)
2) Department for International Development (UK)
3) European Commission (EC)

The external agencies had agreed to fund SSA as an ongoing programme, accepting the existing framework, guidelines and implementation mechanism of the programme.

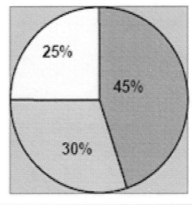

Chart 1. Financing of SSA expenditure.

The total funding was around USD one billion (approximately equivalent to Rs. 4700 crore) and was to cover the period 2003-04 to 2007. The external funds received were to be merged with the domestic funds of the Ministry and the State Governments leaving no dedicated external fund for any particular activity or any geographical area. The external funding was to be based on reimbursement of actual expenditure incurred over and above the threshold level of domestic resources. It was noticed that during 2003-04, external assistance to the tune of Rs. 286.65 crore was received from DFID (Rs. 164.90 crore) and EC (Rs. 121.75 crore) for projects across the whole of India. Against the reimbursement claims amounting to Rs. 580.50 crore lodged during 2004-05 with IDA (Rs. 278.64 crore), DFID (Rs. 191.56 crore) and EC (Rs. 110.30 crore), the claim of Rs. 110.30 crore was outstanding as of December 2005. More effective monitoring and follow up would have enabled the Ministry to avail the reimbursement of Rs. 110.30 crore much before December 2005 which would have helped in enhancing the coverage of SSA. The Ministry was to provide financial assistance to the State Implementation Society (SIS) based on the approved Annual Work Plan and Budget (AWPandB) each year. The details of approved AWPandB, budget allocations and expenditure as indicated in Table 1 given below.

The outlay was to be approved by the Project Approval Board (PAB) of the Department of Elementary Education and Literacy on the basis of plans submitted by SIS.

Table 1. Budget estimates, Revised estimates, Approved outlays, Grants released and Actual expenditure (Rs. in crore)

Year	Budget Estimates*	Revised Estimates*	Outlays approved GOI Share	Outlays approved State Govt. Share	Grants Released by GOI	Grants Released by States	Actual Expenditure
2001-02	500.00	500.00	940.42	165.96	498.68	85.81	172.04
2002-03	1512.00	1220.03	2310.08	770.02	1559.23	414.70	1305.66
2003-04	1951.25	2732.32	6410.65	2136.89	2703.98	874.77	3057.48
2004-05	3057.08	4753.63	8337.66	2779.20	5118.81	1727.58	6598.39
Total			17998.81	5825.07	9880.70	3102.86	11133.57

Source - Budget expenditure Vol. II (notes on Demands for Grants).

Details in Table 1would reveal that the approved budget estimates/revised estimates were far less than the outlay approved by PAB. The revised estimates ranged between 43 *per cent* and 57 *per cent* of the approved outlay during the period 2001-02 to 2004-05. Funds released (Rs. 12983.56 crore) by the Ministry and respective State Governments were far less than the outlay approved (Rs. 23850.88 crore) by PAB.

Examination revealed that though the programme was planned to be taken up earnestly and seriously by the Ministry, it was expected to achieve rather ambitious targets which required enormous funding and serious commitment on the part of the implementing agencies including state governments. Funding requirements approved by PAB which also consisted of representatives from the Ministry, were on the higher side but the funding was slashed at the time of final allotment, which had the potential of adversely affecting the overall implementation of SSA. The budget allocation and release of grants to SIS were much below the amounts required as per AWPandB. This indicated that the work plans were not fully funded by Government. On the contrary, Audit also noticed that the three states *Mizoram* and *Tripura* (as on March 2005) and *Madhya Pradesh* (as on March 2004) could not even spend the funds allotted and had unspent balance amounting to Rs. 35.54 crore. The Ministry had, however, successfully obtained an increase of allocation in revised estimates of 40 *per cent* in 2003-04 and 55 *per cent* in 2004-05, compared to respective BEs though this increased amount was still short of respective approved outlays by 57 *per cent* and 43 *per cent* in the two years.

The Ministry stated that PAB approved higher outlays than the budget allocation approved by Parliament, taking into account the likely low performance of some interventions due to unforeseen constraints such as floods, elections and court interventions. The position of funds released (Government of India and state share) and expenditure there against during the year 2001-02 to 2004-05 was at variance with the position of releases/expenditure forwarded by the States. This indicated that the Ministry and the States did not maintain the data properly and in a uniform manner. Though the States/UTs together were able to spend around 86 *per cent* of the funds released, in some states, the percentage utilization of funds was very poor. The achievement of the objectives of the scheme was also not commensurate with the expenditure incurred as discussed in the ensuing paragraphs. The Ministry replied that there was a shortfall in expenditure in the initial years 2001-02 and 2002-03, as the states had neither adequate experience nor the required staff to run the projects properly. The Ministry further stated that the unutilized funds did not lapse at the end of the year and the funds were allowed to be carried forward to the next year's plan.

2.4.3. Delay in Release of Grants

The manual of 'Financial Management and Procurement' (FMP) stipulated that the Ministry would release funds directly to the State Implementing Society (SIS) in two installments, namely, in April and September every year. The financial norms of the programme further envisaged that the participating state would contribute the agreed ratio of the programme cost within 30 days of the receipt of the contribution of the Union Government as per the approved sharing arrangement. However it was noticed that the Ministry did not release its share as per the prescribed norms as indicated in Table 2.

Thus, during the period 2001-02 to 2004-05, in 66 cases the first installment of the grant was released in the month of September when the second installment should have been released. Similarly, in 31 cases second installment of grant was released in the month of March i.e. at the fag end of the year to avoid the lapse of funds, which did not allow expenditure to be incurred in the same financial year.

Table 2. Summarized position of delay in release of funds

Year	First installment released in the month of September and onwards (No. of states)	Second installment released in the month of March (No. of states)
2001-02	19	5
2002-03	22	10
2003-04	13	5
2004-05	12	11
Total	66	31

The Ministry stated that delay in release of first installment was due to the backlog in release of state share. Further, as the funds (Revised Estimate) were made available at the fag end in March between 2001-02 and 2004-05, second installments could only be released in March. It further stated (June 2006) that from the second year onwards the release of funds to SIS was based on fulfillment of the conditions of release of matching state share, incurring expenditure of at least 50 *per cent* of the available funds and submission of utilization certificates for the year due. The first Joint Review Mission comprised 20 members drawn from various sources (10 from Government of India, 5 from World Bank, 3 from DFID and 2 from European Commission) had also commented that for a variety of reasons such as short release/delayed release of its share by state governments and non availability of electronic transfer system, funds had not flowed as per the prescribed calendar causing slippage in the achievement of programme targets.

2.4.4. Utilization Certificates

Utilization certificates (UCs) from districts to the national mission through the states in respect of the first installment of a particular year were required to be furnished at the time of release of the first installment of the subsequent year. There was to be no further release if utilization certificates were not submitted as per the schedule.

2.4.5. Diversion of Funds and other Financial Irregularities

Audit examination revealed that during the period 2001-05, funds amounting to Rs. 99.88 crore were diverted from SSA for meeting expenditure not covered under the scheme in eleven states of which, the state spend Rs. 18.13 crore citing causes like Uniforms to girl students of primary schools, purchase of crockery and utensils for mid day meal scheme, purchase of computers, air conditioners, typewriters, Xerox, fax machine, mobile phones, repair of bungalow etc. The Ministry stated that funds were utilized for SSA activities with the aim of universalization of elementary education in the state. The reply is not tenable, as all the reported expenditure could not be covered under SSA.

Apart from the above diversion of funds, other irregularities like unspent amounts and incurring expenditure beyond delegated powers involving Rs. 472.51 crore in 14 states/union territories were noticed in audit.

2.5. HUMAN RESOURCE

In order to have an optimum teacher-student ratio, SSA norms provided for one teacher for every 40 students in primary and upper primary school and at least two teachers in a primary school and one teacher for every class in the upper primary school. Examination of records in the states revealed discrepancies which are indicated in the table given below (Source: Ministry of Human Resource Development, Department of Elementary Education and Literacy, Performance audit report on 'Sarva Shiksha Abhiyan').

2.5.1. Deployment of Teachers in Schools

Chhattisgarh, Himachal Pradesh, Gujarat, Madhya Pradesh, Punjab, Uttar Pradesh and West Bengal 6647 schools did not have any teacher. In West Bengal, the process of engaging para teachers had started on the basis of High Court orders *Jharkhand* and *West Bengal* 96 schools with 264 teachers but not even a single student was enrolled.

As the shortages were not insignificant these would have adversely affected the imparting of useful and relevant education to the targeted children. Excess teachers in some states/districts indicated lack of monitoring/administrative control.

2.5.2. Opening of Schools/Alternative Schooling Facility

As per the norms, new primary schools were to be opened only in those areas, which did not have any school within one km of a habitation. EGS centers at primary level were to be opened in unserved habitations where no school existed within a radius of one km and there were at least 15 children in the age group of 6-14 years who were not going to school. Audit scrutiny revealed that in the State of West Bengal, out of 3794 total no. of habitations, 1617 i.e. 42.62 percentage of habitations were without schools. The Ministry replied that primary schools or EGS centers had been opened subsequently in 2005-06 resulting in downward trend in school less habitation.

Existence of large number of habitations without schools indicated lack of proper planning and survey by SIS/state governments, which not only deprived the children of the benefit of the scheme in the habitations but also adversely affected attainment of the objectives of SSA. It also underlined the need for the Ministry to decide a specific strategy to monitor the progress closely.

2.5.3. Opening of Upper Primary Schools

As per the norms, new upper primary schools were to be opened based on the number of children completing primary education, upto a ceiling of one upper primary school/section for every two primary schools. Test check of records revealed a shortage of 54.47 *per cent* upper primary schools. Of the total 25127 number of schools required, shortage of upper primary schools in the state was 13687.

Table 3. Discrepancies relating to deployment of teachers

S.No.	Name of the state	Discrepancy noticed	Ministry's comments
1	Assam, Chhattisgarh, Himachal Pradesh, Gujarat, Jharkhand, Karnataka, Maharashtra, Manipur, Orissa, Punjab, Rajasthan, Tripura, Uttar Pradesh, West Bengal and Dadra and Nagar Haveli	75884 schools with only one teacher	The Ministry replied (June 2006) that some states had a policy for providing a single teacher in schools, with an enrolment of less than 20 or 15 children in sparsely populated regions and hilly areas
2	Chhattisgarh, Himachal Pradesh, Gujarat, Madhya Pradesh, Punjab, Uttar Pradesh and West Bengal	6647 schools did not have any teacher	In Punjab, the ban imposed on recruitment of teachers had since been lifted. In U.P. efforts were being made to have minimum 4 teachers in each school by March 2006. In West Bengal, the
3	Jharkhand and West Bengal	96 schools with 264 teachers but not even a single student was enrolled	No comments
4	Andhra Pradesh, Chattisgarh, Gujarat, Jharkhand, Madhya Pradesh, Orissa (17 districts), Punjab, Tripura and West Bengal	Shortage of 2.23 lakh teachers	No Comments
5	Assam, Meghalaya and Orissa (13 districts)	74256 excess teachers	-do-
6	Bihar	Ratio of teacher student ratio alarmingly high (Primary: 1:60, Upper Primary 1:130)	-do-
7	Jharkhand and Uttaranchal	Teacher student ratio was 1:57	-do-
8	Rajasthan	Teacher student ratio was 1:45 to 1:79	-do-
9	Uttar Pradesh	Teacher student ratio was 1:76	-do-

2.5.4. Supply of Free Textbooks to Focus Group Children

The scheme envisaged that free textbooks within an upper ceiling of Rs. 150 per child would be provided to all children in the focus group namely girl child and SC/ST children. States were to continue to fund free textbooks being currently provided from the State Plans. In such cases, free textbooks under SSA should not be provided to the focus group children. In case subsidy was partially provided, assistance under SSA was to be restricted to that portion of the cost of books, which was being borne by the children. Instances of erroneous supply of books were noticed by audit as detailed. During 2001-02, in *West Bengal*, focus group children in five test checked districts were not provided with textbooks.

2.5.5. Maintenance and Repairs of School Buildings

Grant under this component of SSA was available only to those schools, which had existing buildings of their own. Specific proposal by the school committee had to be submitted and community contribution was to be ensured. Schools with three classrooms and more than three classrooms were eligible for maintenance grant of Rs. 4000 and Rs. 7500 respectively per school per year keeping the overall limit for the district at Rs. 5000 per school. Government aided schools or other private schools were outside the scope of these provisions. Audit scrutiny revealed that in *Assam, Bihar, Himachal Pradesh, Orissa, Rajasthan, Tamil Nadu* and *West Bengal, Rs.* 128.13 crore was disbursed without specific proposals from VECs. In *West Bengal* Rs. 1.17 crore was paid to 771 to 801 schools during 2002-05, which were not housed in their in own buildings. A proper monitoring system would have prevented grants from being released to ineligible schools, excess release of grants, and utilization of funds for unintended purposes.

2.5.6. Training for Upgrading Teachers' Skills

To upgrade the skills of teachers, the SSA provides for in-service course for 20 days for all teachers each year, refresher course for untrained teachers already employed as teachers for 60 days and orientation for 30 days for freshly trained recruits. Audit scrutiny revealed that as on 31 March 2005, of the total no. of teachers i.e. 535956 in the state, 406150 i.e. 75.78 percentage of teachers were not provided any training. Either training was not organized at all during a particular year or it was not imparted for the full duration.

The Ministry stated that in principle, 20 days' teacher training was being approved for the states for the existing teachers every year. However, the states provided training to teachers taking into account the fact that there should be minimum disturbance in classroom transaction and they should not be away from the classrooms for many days. Thus, the target of upgrading professional skills of teachers was not achieved. However, differences were noticed in the data as reported by some states and those reported by the Ministry. This showed that data regarding trained/untrained teachers was not properly maintained at the state and national levels, which hampered up gradation of professional skills of around 42 *per cent* teachers. No performance evaluation of the teachers, after the training was taken up. In some government middle schools, the pass percentage was even zero. The Ministry stated that during 2001-02, no training programme could be organized being the first year of SSA implementation. The school results depended upon a number of factors many of which were out of control of the implementing agencies. The teachers appointed were below the required minimum education level. The Ministry stated that distance education-training programme for duration of six months through IGNOU was being imparted to untrained teachers under SSA.

2.5.7. Training of Community Leaders

At least four community leaders per village plus two persons per school in a year were to be provided two days' training per year at the rate of Rs. 30 per day per person. In urban areas where no village existed and in states where revenue village covered a vast area, training to three community leaders per school was envisaged. It was noticed that in *Arunachal Pradesh, Maharashtra, Nagaland, Tripura, West Bengal, Dadra and Nagar Haveli, Daman and Diu, Delhi* and *Lakshadweep*, outlay was approved for community leaders' training but no training was imparted. In *Maharashtra, Nagaland, Tripura* and *West Bengal*, Rs. 3.01 crore was spent but no training was imparted. The survey conducted by SRI at the instance of audit disclosed that only 59.3 *per cent* primary schools, 24.4 *per cent* upper primary schools and 7.7 *per cent* of high schools with upper primary schools had education committees and in only 64.3 *per cent* of schools, the community members had been trained.

2.5.8. Management Cost

As per the norms of SSA, the total management cost should be less than 6 *per cent* of the total cost, separately for each district and also in totality for the entire state. No new permanent post was to be created. The vacancies should be filled up only through contract or through deputation. No permanent liability should accrue on the society or the state government due to filling up of these posts. Deputation allowance was also not allowed for posts filled on deputation basis.

The Ministry stated that management cost was not to be calculated on the ceiling of 6 per cent based on actual expenditure. It was to be computed on the outlay approved. The Ministry's reply is not tenable as the management cost computed with reference to the outlay was the ceiling upto which it could be incurred. The actual cost had to be worked out with reference to the actual expenditure incurred, which was often much less than the outlay. Even the funds released by the Ministry in almost all the cases were less than the outlay.

2.5.9 Block Resources Centers (BRC)/Cluster Resource Centers (CRC)

SSA envisaged establishment of BRCs/CRCs as resource centers catering to a group of schools subject to specific norms for professional upgradation of primary school teachers by conducting various in-service training programmes at the block level. These BRCs/CRCs were to be located in the school campus as far as possible with 20 Block Resource Persons (BRP) for blocks with more than 100 schools and 10 BRPs for smaller blocks. It has been revealed that hardly any work had been done under this intervention. There were many deficiencies in setting up of BRCs/CRCs. In **West Bengal,** against 5636 Resource Teachers, only 1915 were deployed as of March 2005. The Ministry stated that efforts were being made to bridge the gap and to engage more resource teachers. The Ministry further added that it was decided to utilize the unspent amount of salaries of BRCs and CRCs for providing necessary infrastructure to schools. Construction of BRCs/CRCs had to be abandoned as the ceiling of Rs. 2 lakh per unit was stated to be a constraint and there was escalation in the cost of construction. Thus, the Ministry itself admitted diversion of funds, incorrect accounting and reporting.

2.6. Results of the Government's Efforts to Enroll Identified/Target Group Children Back to School (Out of School Children)

The primary objective of SSA was to enroll all children in the age group of 6-14 years in schools, education guarantee centers (EGC), alternative schools and back to school camps (BSC) by 2003. The target for achieving this goal was modified (23 March 2005) by the National Commission from 2003 to 2005. At the commencement of the scheme the number of out of school children in the age group of 6-14 years on 1 April 2001 was 3.40 crore children. On 31 March 2005, after four years of implementation of the scheme and after having incurred an expenditure of Rs. 11133.57 crore by the Ministry/State Governments, 1.36 crore (40 *per cent*) children still remained out of school. Thus, neither was the original goal of all children in school by 2003 nor the revised target of bringing all children in school by 2005 was achieved. This deprived a large number of the targeted children of the intended benefit under SSA. This would imply that either the deadlines set initially were over ambitious or the funding was inadequate or the implementation needed to be strengthened.

2.6.1. Achievements: Some Highlights

Several states have started exercises aimed at improving the levels of basic learning achievement on state-wide scale. Many pilots are now being scaled up state-wide. Most notable among these is the Tamil Nadu Activity Based Learning program. The Mission was also happy to see specific goal setting towards achievement of basic reading, writing, and math skills at every standard as represented by Himachal Pradesh. Combining overall improvement in classroom processes, teacher capacity building, and focus on basic skills learning is important.

Increased focus on quality on education from the fact that SSA conducted studies on teacher absence, students' attendance, students' time on task, and parateachers. This is commendable and the findings of the latter two studies are awaited with interest.

The proportion of out of school children in the 6-13 age group, computed on the basis of door to door annual surveys by teachers, is reported to have dropped to about 3.5% (about 70 lac children) in 2004-05 and more or less stagnant (about 75 lac children) in 2006-07 against an independently verified proportion of about **6.94%** in September 2005.

Gender gap is reported to be dropping steadily. Operationalization of the Kasturba Gandhi Balika Vidyalayas are a major step forward in SSA as is indicated by the field review report. Its merger with SSA in the 11th plan is a very welcome step.

The dropout rates too continue to decline except in about 97 districts where they are stagnant. The national dropout rates before completing primary stage have dropped from 14.9% to 10.39% between 2002-03 and 2005-06. Simultaneously, the transition rates from primary to upper primary stage have risen by about 10 percentage points to 83.36%. This progress indicates that all children entering schools today could complete at least full eight years of education.

The program for Children with Special Needs is particularly important. It is reaching out to ever larger numbers of children and involves larger number of NGOs than previous years. Nearly 2.4 million children have been identified and about 2 million of these covered either through mainstreaming into schools or through home-based education with an involvement of 6,687 resource teachers and 687 NGOs.

The goals for provisioning of new schools, classrooms, toilets etc are being met to the extent of 91% with 67% completion and the rest in process. It is projected that the infrastructure gap in all except about 5 states will be insignificant, if any, by the end of 2007-08. Provision of a primary school within 1 km of 98% population is a gigantic achievement despite the unevenness. Similarly a primary school to upper primary school ratio of 2.61: 1, which is further declining favorably is also heartening news.

The District Information System for Education, DISE, which was initiated in seven states in 1994-95, has now expanded to cover all 35 states and UT's. More importantly, the time lag between data gathering and reporting has reduced dramatically. A couple of years ago the time lag was over two years. This Mission could get information for 2006-07 for 25 states at the beginning of the academic year 2007-08. Also, comparison with other sources of information indicates that the reliability of the data too has improved considerably. Several states including Orissa, Karnataka, and Himachal have moved beyond DISE to creating their own individual child database, which are used for tracking.

The MHRD Bureau's data and also fund allocations have increasingly become more district, and even block-specific over the last year. It is good to see even cluster-specific data indicting considerable improvement in micro-level planning. This is a major gain, which has clearly helped in targeting issues of unevenness that are often hidden under good overall figures. This is especially true of equity issues related the girl child, SC/ST, and minorities. SSA has identified districts and blocks which have concentration of problems related to these social categories and extra efforts are being made supported by additional funding and flexible programs. These strategies should start yielding results in a short while.

Chapter 3

THE SCENARIO OF WEST BENGAL

The world celebrated September 8 as International Literacy Day but a look at the state of schools in West Bengal — and we find that they have little to hurrah about. Nagendranath Mondal is the headmaster of the Ramchandrapur Ashutosh Primary School in the suburb of Bally in Howrah district either. He is, instead, worried about not being able to provide tables and chairs for his teachers and students. "It is the lack of basic facilities that really bothers us here," he says, pointing to the tiny room that passes for a classroom, where students from class I to IV all study together. "The space is too small but we do not have sufficient funds to expand," he rues. The roof leaks and the school are often hijacked by political parties for meetings. In the midst of all that, Mondal has to strive to keep his students — most of who come from poor families — from dropping out of school.

But Mondal's situation is not unique. Half a decade after the launch of the Central government's grandiose Sarva Shiksha Abhiyan (SSA) to eliminate illiteracy and four years after economist Amartya Sen's non-governmental organization (NGO) Pratichi Trust made embarrassing revelations about primary education in West Bengal; the state of education continues to be in a shambles in the Left Front-ruled state. Though the SSA sought to educate all students in the 5-14 age group by 2010, West Bengal has been lagging behind in spreading the education net. According to a handbook of the West Bengal state SSA, almost 39 lakh children have either dropped out of school, or have not taken admission. According to a recent statement in Parliament by the human resource development ministry, the dropout rate for students in West Bengal studying in class I to X is 80 per cent (the state government contests this figure), considerably higher than the national rate of 52 per cent.

The situation is poor in most parts of India where 1.36 crore children, or 40 per cent of the total 3.40 crore, are still out of school. But West Bengal — with Chhattisgarh, Himachal Pradesh, Gujarat, Madhya Pradesh, Punjab and Uttar Pradesh is among the worst offenders. And many believe that one of the main reasons for the abysmal state of affairs is the paucity of teachers. "The pay scale is dismal for SSA teachers. Some teachers are paid as little as Rs 1,000 a month," says Brendan McCarthaigh, an SSA teacher trainer and head of Students Empowerment Rights and Vision Through Education (SERVE), a Calcutta-based NGO that works in the field of education. Inadequate pay, he argues, leads to dismal standards of teaching.

Under the SSA, the teacher-student ratio should be 1:40. Officially the situation is not all that bad in the state. According to statistics provided by the government of India, the teacher-student ratio is 1:52 in primary schools in West Bengal, 1:36 in the elementary schools and 1:41 in secondary schools. But as a quick tour of some schools indicates, the situation is alarming. Mohammed Jarjis Ali, a teacher at the Osmania High Madrassa in Malda district, holds that the ratio in his school — and several other schools — is closer to 1:100. "In our institution, we lack both teaching and non-teaching staff," says Ali. A poor teacher-student ratio leads to high dropout rates. "If a school does not have enough teachers, students automatically drop out," says Mondal of the Ramchandrapur Ashutosh Primary School. "It is difficult to get deprived children to study because of deep-rooted stereotypes among parents who dismiss education," he says.

Lack of funds is a common complaint, but a report by the Comptroller and Auditor General of India (CAG) in the year 2005-06 shows that West Bengal received Rs 341 crore for SSA, more than double of the Rs 167.48 crore it got in 2003-2004. But the CAG points out that the money has not always been spent on education. Officials, however, are reluctant to condemn the scheme. "It is true that the SSA has some way to go to ensure total literacy in the state, but to say that it is a complete failure is like throwing the baby out with the bath water," says a senior official of the community mobilisation and alternative education section of the West Bengal government's department of school education. At the ground level, though, the indications are that education is in a mess. Many district schools do not have proper infrastructure and quite a few do not have adequate sitting arrangements for students. Sweltering in the summer heat in a cramped room is quite the norm. "Our teachers have even donated money to bring electricity to our school since we have not received a government grant (for this)," says Sukumar Ghosh, headmaster of the Durgapur Pallimangal Primary School in Bally. Teachers are also concerned that students of different classes are taught in the same room simultaneously. "One room for four classes is woefully inadequate for both students and teachers, for it becomes really tough to tackle children of several classes all at once," says Sadhana Kundu, a teacher at the Durgapur Pallimangal School.

And while the usually acclaimed mid-day meal scheme — under which students are given a simple meal in school — is meant to increase attendance, lack of space leads to a situation where they are forced to have their meals in the classroom itself. "While the scheme is good per se, there are problems in proper implementation owing to the unavailability of separate rooms for meals," says Ghosh. Parents, clearly, are not happy with the quality of education either. The parents of seven-year-old Sulemina Khatun pulled her out of the Osmania Madrassa in Malda. Her mother, Fatima Bibi, felt she was wasting her time in school. "I would rather have her work than recite poetry," says Fatima. The bottomline of any educational scheme is to reach children. What do they have to say about the so-called institutions of enlightenment? "I would like to have more books and pencils," says eight-year-old Sushobhan Sen, a class IV student at the Durgapur Pallimangal School. Sen likes his teachers and enjoys reading Rabindranath Tagore — but there are times when he feels all boxed in. School, for many like him, is almost like a sentence.

Chapter 4

RESULTS OF THE PRIMARY FIELD SURVEY

To gather information, field survey is the most convenient and faithful way. We decided to do survey of 10 schools, but due to unavoidable circumstances we could cover only 9 schools in which we got 7 schools with both primary and secondary and 2 schools having only primary section. In each school, 10 students (we have interviewed 5 students each from primary and secondary section in every school) and 2 teachers have been interviewed. This leads to a total of 80 students comprising of 45 primary students and 35 secondary students. Moreover, we interviewed 17 teachers from various schools. Qualitative method is used for this project. It helps in probing the sub-conscious mind of the respondent. For this project, we designed 4 types of questionnaire. First type is for students from class 1-5, second one is for class 6-8; third one for teachers and the last one are for SSA officers. Questionnaire design is a vital issue in interviewing. A properly designed questionnaire can tap the necessary information from the respondent. Questionnaires fall under various categories, such as structured, unstructured, disguised and undisguised. Our questionnaires were prepared based one unstructured concept where we have kept open-ended questions to probe into the mind of respondent, allowing the interviewee to express his own thoughts rather than restricting him to the available response options.

Total questionnaire has been divided into several parts. Even for getting specific responses we have enhanced some options for upper primary questionnaires. Mainly the students' questionnaire is divided into 5 parts (attached as an annexure):

- How much a student is involved in the schooling process
- Interaction within class/ measurement of quality education
- Teaching aids used
- Infrastructure
- Aids from the government

In the teachers' questionnaire, questions are regarding

- Work load
- School's initiative regarding drop-out students
- Reasons for dropping-out
- Quality of education etc.

The interviewers consciously guided the interviewee through a sequential, pre-formulated set of tactful questions to extract the 'factual' responses, minimizing on influencing factors. In the following we have stated our finding at length by comprehensively analyzing the data that we got during the survey.

4.1. STUDENTS' SURVEY REPORT

This section mainly deals with the allocation of teachers in schools in the Kolkata region and the feelings of the students towards their teacher.

Involvement with schooling process	Number (%age)
Liking Academics	19 (23.75)
Liking non-academics	12 (15)
Liking both academics and non-academics	44 (55)
Dislike/Fear	5 (6.25)
Total students	80 (100)

From the above we can easily conclude the students will become much more involved with the schooling process if they get both academics and non-academics properly.

Whether a teacher is asking questions to his/her students	Number (%age)
Yes	78 (97.5)
Sometimes	2 (2.5)
No	0 (0)
Total students interviewed	80 (100)

Near about 98% students told that their teachers ask questions to them. It is showing that quality of education has enhanced.

Whether teacher is responding to queries raised by students	Number (%age)
Yes	78 (97.5)
Sometimes	1 (1.25)
No	1 (1.25)
Total students interviewed	80 (100)

4.1.1. Frequency of Assessment

Frequency of assessment is same everywhere. Total 8 unit tests and one 100 marks test have been taken through out the year. Among 8 tests, 4 tests of 20 marks and remaining 4 tests of 10 marks are taken in every consecutive month. But some students have told that sometime school authority takes 1 test of 25 marks instead of 2 consecutive 10 and 20 marks tests.

This new type of assessment system has been started to properly judge a student but sometime school authority is taking 2 exams together to make their task easy. If proper monitoring has not been done, then this new system will not work properly.

Whether you (being) a student ask questions to your teachers or not	Number (%age)
Yes	69 (86.25)
Sometimes	8 (10)
No	3 (3.75)
Total students interviewed	80 (100)

From the above diagram we can easily conclude that student's interaction with teacher in a class has reached a satisfactory level.

Reason for asking questions	Number (%age)
Don't understand	54 (79.4)
Inattentive	14 (20.6)
Total students interviewed	68 (100)

4.2. TEACHING AIDS

4.2.1. Black board, Chalks, Dusters

All schools are using black board, chalks and dusters as teaching aid irrespective of primary and upper primary students. Only 71.11% primary students and 77.14% upper primary students has told that charts and maps are used as teaching aids where as in case of upper primary students every one should be taught with charts and maps. Very few schools take their students for educational excursions.

4.2.2. Charts and Maps

In all the schools charts and maps are used to teach biology, geography etc. And for primary classes charts are used to teach flora and fauna.

	Primary	Upper Primary
Yes	32 (71.11)	27 (77.14)
Sometimes	6 (13.33)	5 (14.29)
No	7 (15.55)	3 (8.57)
Total Students interviewed	45 (100)	35 (100)

4.2.3. Models

Two primary schools namely Adi Mahakali Patshala and Shanti Sangha Siksha Mandir did not use any kind of models for the teaching purpose. On the other hand schools having secondary section used different kind of models for teaching.

	Primary	Upper Primary
Yes	0 (0)	5 (14.29)
Sometimes	0 (0)	3 (8.57)
No	35 (100)	27 (77.14)
Total Students interviewed	35 (100)	35 (100)

4.2.4. Interface with Nature (Excursion Type)

Interface with nature and extracurricular activities: Only three schools out of nine has gone for any kind of interface with nature i.e. excursion over last one year. It should be noted that Siksha Niketan for Girls was found out to be only school that has an active extracurricular part in their education process... which includes excursions, role play, youth parliament and sports competition. Among 9 schools, only 2 schools have taken their students to educational excursions.

4.3. INFRASTRUCTURE

4.3.1. Playground and Play Material

The only school that had a playground and provides play material to the student was Oriental Seminary, though play materials were insufficient. Apart from this Shanti Sangha Siksha Mandir had a playground but no play materials, and Siksha Niketan for Girls gives insufficient indoor play materials to the girls but has no playground. So, we can see that all the other six schools neither have a playground nor provide any play materials. Only 2 schools have playground within the school campus among 9 schools wherever we have interviewed i.e only near about 22% schools have their own playground.

4.3.2. Playing Material

Maximum schools don't have sufficient amount of playing materials for students.

4.3.3. Drinking Water

Drinking water is another major concern for SSA. In the table 4 given below we can see the source of supply of water to different school. Moreover, it is pleasing to see that at least three schools are using electric water purification system for drinking water. Here among 9 schools 8 schools have overhead reservoir but students don't know after how many days those reservoirs are cleaned.

Table 4. Water Supply Source of Schools

Source	Number
Electric Water Purifier	3
Overhead Reservoir	4
Tap Water (direct)	2
Tube Well	0

Toilet cleaned: From the Pie Chart (Figure 2) we can see that toilets are seldom cleaned in most of the schools, in only three schools toilets are cleaned on a daily basis, there is a school where toilets were never cleaned and in the rest schools toilets are seldom cleaned. These unhygienic and unhealthy toilets may lead to various kinds of contagious diseases. We also came to know that in some schools the separate toilets for teachers are very clean but the toilets for students are exactly opposite. This shows the look down upon approach of the school authorities towards the students.

4.3.4. Frequency of Cleaning Toilets in Various Schools

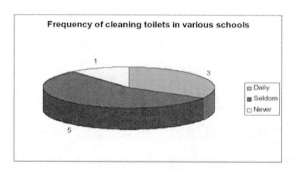

Figure 3.

Even in case of toilets also, cleanliness of toilets is a major part of concern. Here among 9 schools, only in 3 schools students told that toilets are cleaned regularly.

Government should form a monitoring group who will take care of all these infrastructure related problems. Only alloting fund will not be sufficient for SSA to achieve their target. Proper field work should be done to make the program successful.

4.3.5. Spaciousness of the Classrooms

As far as classrooms are considered all the schools have been rated either good or average for capaciousness. They all have desk and bench for the seating arrangement and are very decent (Figure 4).

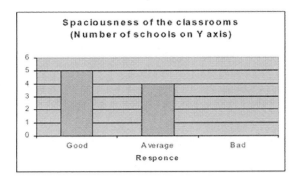

Figure 4.

4.4. AIDS FROM GOVERNMENT

4.4.1. Timely Availability of Books

In all the primary classes (i.e. till standard V) of the schools books are supplied from the government. As the quantity of books supplied is insufficient... the schools authorities at times shortlist very needy students, and are given priority when books are distributed. So, a large number of students are left with only a few books and they have to buy the rest. In addition, hardly any book is given to secondary students... they have to buy all the books and in some schools students use the library to fulfil their need.

	Primary	Upper primary
Yes	40 (88.89)	15 (42.86)
No	5 (11.11)	20 (57.14)
Number of students surveyed	45 (100)	35 (100)

Data of Timely availability of books for upper primary students are pathetically low. These data are showing that funds are not properly utilized.

4.4.2. Notebooks/Copies

Copies are not supplied by the government to any school. Often, stationeries are donated by NGOs or corporate houses to some of the schools. Students did not get any copy from government.

4.4.3. Health Check up

During the last one year health check up is done only once in four of the schools. One of the school follows unorthodox style of doing check up, there students are given coupons to pay visit to a common doctor whenever needed. We also came to know that in some schools the school authorities themselves does the medical of the students… which raises the question of reliability and privacy (of the students) of these medical checkups.

	Primary	Upper Primary
Yes	15 (33.33)	15 (24.86)
No	30 (66.67)	20 (57.14)
Number of students surveyed	45 (100)	35 (100)

4.4.4. Feedback of Teachers on the Quality of the Books Supplied by the Government

Out of the 17 teachers interviewed, 7 teachers have rated the books to be Very Good, 4 teachers consider it to be Good and 4 consider it to be Fair, only two have rated the quality to be excellent and none of them believe it to be Poor. So, we can say that the government has done very well as far as the quality and content of the books are considered (Figure 5).

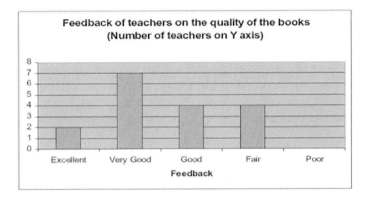

Figure 5.

4.5. TEACHERS' SURVEY REPORT: (RESPONDING SCHOOLS ONLY)

Name of the school	Avg, no. of classes per week	Avg, no. of students per class	Pupil-Teacher ratio
Adi Mahakali Pathsala	28	95	42.23:1
Ahiritola Banga Vidyalaya	28-30	40	12:1
Beleghata Deshbandhu Vidyapith	30	50	31:1
Kishore Bidyapith	26-28	88	30:1
Oriental Seminary	25	30	12:1
Purba Kolkata Vidyatan	26	18	20:1
Kankurgachi Vivekananda Vidyapith	24-25	50	35:1

4.5.1. Work Load

Number of classes per teacher per week is more or less equal.

4.5.2. Average Number of Students Per Class

Average number of students per class is different in different schools and the range is widely distributed. One school has 18-20 students per class where as other school has 80-90 students. Government should look after why in some schools average no. of students is low.

4.5.3. Teacher-Student Ratio

The optimum teacher-student ratio according to SSA norm is 1:40. In the table given below teacher-student ratio for the schools are given (table 4). From the above data we can see that only Adi Mahakali Patshala has a teacher-student ratio of 1:42, which is violating the SSA norm.

Steps taken by different schools to attract new students/ old drop-out students:

- Arranging teacher-parents meetings
- Deducting all educational charges for needy students
- Arranging different types of educational campaign

Perceptions of Teachers:

- Only by providing books, attracting students is not possible
- If government can arrange mid-day meal in Kolkata then some students can be attracted
- Thorough survey should be done by government to know the actual scenario of different schools
- Government should change the hierarchical architecture of SSA Framework to make it more successful

Chapter 5

QUALITATIVE ANALYSIS

5.1. RELATED TO INFRASTRUCTURE PRESENT IN GOVERNMENT SCHOOLS IN KOLKATA

- Schools get money from Sarva Siksha on the basis of what they need in terms of infrastructure. But most of the time the money allotted to a particular school cannot be utilized and the whole money goes back to the respective authority. Suppose a sum of money is allotted to construct a class room on the first floor of a school building. The money is allotted on the basis of size of the classroom and other factors. But it is difficult for the respective school authority to spent that money and construct one class room due to the reason that Sarva Siksha will not give any financial help to construct the staircase which will lead to that particular class room which is located on the first floor of a school building. In most of the cases the respective schools don't have enough funds to construct a staircase on their own, so as a result of which they cannot construct the class room on the first floor, and the whole allotted money is taken back after a certain time by the respective Sarva Siksha authorities.
- Most of the school authorities interviewed for the purpose, said that the respective school heads have to bargain a lot in terms of the amount of money that is to be allotted for a purpose. According to them It is a general tendency of the Sarva Siksha Authorities to allot a lesser amount than what is actually need for the purpose. So either the project remains incomplete or the schools spend from their own fund (though rare) to complete a project.

- The Sarva Siksha allots money separately for may be constructing a toilet, or a library or may be for a class room. If the money is allotted for all these construction work at one go for a school who needs all these facilities for it students, its easier for the school authorities to complete the project at one go. Otherwise, individual construction involves a lot of time and effort from the part of the school authorities, which can be utilized for some other fruitful work for the improvement and betterment of the school itself.
- Funds for a purpose are often delayed, so the respective schools face a lot of problem.
- Most of the schools are not allotted proper fund as far as maintenance of their old school building is concerned. The school authorities face a lot of problem due to this.
- Schools do complain about unethical practices and the way fund allocation is done
- In all the schools the teachers use separate toilets and they are clean on a regular basis.
- In one of the school we found that the school building is used by the localites for marriage purposes, and due to this reason the Electronic water purifier that is used to purify water has been disconnected temporarily. So students are drinking water directly from the overhead reservoir.

5.2. QUALITATIVE ANALYSIS RELATED TO FACTORS OTHER THAN INFRASTRUCTURE

- In case of books provided by Sarva Siksha, most of the schools don't get them on time, and if they get it at all, either they are fewer in number compared to number of students or damaged to a large extent.
- Many primary schools or even primary section of secondary schools don't have efficient teachers to tackle and handle the children properly, understand their needs and deliver accordingly.
- Most of the time it is seen that students joining a secondary school after completing their primary level learning from a different school, are unable to adjust to this new atmosphere which ultimately lead to large number of drop outs.

- A very common problem that the school authorities face both in the primary and secondary section is frequent dropouts. According to the teachers since their exist no rewards for the students to attend school, so why should they at all turn up to attend a class, rather they will utilize the time to earn something for himself/herself and also for their family. Their should be a reward given to students for attending school daily, like the mid day meal, which is common in government schools in West Bengal other than Kolkata.

Chapter 6

RECOMMENDATIONS

- From the above primary data we can easily understand that there is a problem at the grass-root level. Proper strategic implementation of SSA is not taking place.
- Proper block level data-base should be prepared.
- All schools in West Bengal should be surveyed.
- Proper need of each school should be acknowledged.
- Decentralized decision making framework should be prepared at National level and state level.

6.1. RECOMMENDED FRAMEWORK

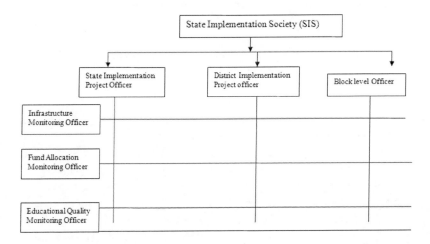

The Under Secretaries and the Section Officers in the Elementary Education Bureau, along with the Office Staff, etc. will be part of the National Mission. In order to facilitate effective monitoring and operational support for MIS, a monitoring and operation support unit will be established from the existing staff and by appointment of a few need-based Consultants as per rules. The management costs approved for the National Mission will be utilised for engaging the Consultants and establishing the monitoring and operational support unit. The operational support unit will work very closely with the National Resource institutions providing the professional support.

The National Mission has a major role to play in developing capacities. In order to facilitate such a process, demand-based capacity development visits would be organized by the National Mission, in consultation with the State Missions. State Missions would also play an important role in meeting the capacity development needs of the districts as per their requirement. The professional and operational support institutions will also regularly interact with State Implementation Societies and districts to ascertain the capacity development needs. Flexibility in meeting the capacity development needs is critical to the success of Sarva Shiksha Abhiyan. The National Mission has the role of disseminating good practices across the states. This will include encouraging Study visits and regularly publishing such good practices. The monitoring and operational support unit of the National Mission will respond to the demand from States and districts. It will have the flexibility of sending monitoring teams at short notice. The National Mission will constantly update lists of experts in functional and geographical areas in consultation with State Implementation Societies. The list of experts would be periodically placed before the Executive Committee for approval.

6.2. Uniform Approach: Putting Money Where it Matters?

SSA has formula based funding pattern with a unified approach without taking into consideration the special needs and context. SSA's district budgets, once approved, equal amounts of funds are transferred to all the blocks. Financial parameters whether it is per child or per facility, e.g., alternative school, are not variable depending on the degree of the educational challenge that states have to contend with. This kind of 'equality' in funding may not help to bring 'equity' in education.

6.3. TARGET CENTERED APPROACH

SSA's has different centers to work as per local demands. But these centers CRC/BRC/DRCs are generally busy in collecting mere data to showcase their achievements in quantifiable terms. The use of funds in the budget are not properly linked to expected outcomes of the associated annual plan for the year. Evidence based programming and result oriented budget framework is no where to be found. As per different review reports of SSA (available on www.ssa.nic.in) the staff involved in special schemes like NPEGEL, KGBVS, mid day meal are hardly aware about the full provisions and guidelines of the programmes. This clearly affects the delivery of programmes at local level.

6.4. ADMINISTRATIVE INEFFICIENCY IN FLOW OF FUNDS

Despite decentralization of planning, very little autonomy is exercised at district and block levels on financial matters, without approval from the top. Lack of timely approval and transfers are known to lead to substantial under-utilization of allocated funds. For example in Haryana in 2004-05, first instalment of Central Share of Rs.5000 lakhs was released on 13.8.04 against which State Share of Rs.1667.00 lakhs was released on 12.10.04, after a delay of two months. The second installment of Rs.7500.00 lakhs was released on 4.2.05 against which no State share has been released up to 21.03.05.

6.5. LEARNING OUTCOMES: WHOSE RESPONSIBILITY?

Learning outcome seems to be nobody's responsibility either at local level or at district or state level. A few weeks ago there were full page ads in the national newspapers about the success of SSA in terms of enrolment, number of schools, teachers, and so on. These aspects (including enrolment) are inputs into the process of education, they are not outcomes. No evidence was provided about whether more children were now able to read, write or do maths as a result of programmes like the SSA. (ASER, 2005 by Pratham, indicates that close to 52% of children could not read a short story at the Standard II level of difficulty).

6.6. Monitoring Gimmicks

Monitoring under the SSA is envisaged as a three tiered one: monitoring at the local community level, at the State level and the National level. A centrally sponsored scheme dealing with the appraisal, approval, funding, monitoring and evaluation of 600+ districts. There is dearth of technical and professional resources at the center geared to meet this challenge adequately. The regional institutions are not equipped and capable of supporting the Center in these efforts. Diets are invisible in their functioning at local level.

A range of educational processes would benefit from a screening for 'value for money' under SSA. Involvement of local authorities in the review process will definitely go beyond quantifiable targets used to review and monitor. For example if we take teachers training – given the very substantial resources allocated for teacher training, and the nature of mobilization that takes place to carry out mass in-service teacher training programs there is very little evidence on what this is bringing to schools and children. Much of the monitoring concentrates on only number of teachers trained per state per year - were they new teachers or old? Did they get different modules of teacher training? Did the same teacher receive training each year while others did not? Did the teacher training programs add concrete professional skills to teachers each time? Do they address varying degrees of professional competence among teachers? In addition, most importantly what was the impact of teacher training in schools and on children's learning and achievement levels? Without such information, the value of money spent cannot be judged.

SSA provides guidelines to the states for local adaptation of the programme and schemes. Most of the states have not done so. Disfunctionality of committees and authorities to implement the programme also serves as weakness to the programme. For example, as per the joint review report of Haryana, 2005, after the formation of the Haryana Prathmik Shiksha Pariyojna Parishad (HPSPP) in March 1993 as an autonomous and independent society under the Registration of Societies Act, 1860, the implementation of SSA in Haryana was entrusted to this society (HPSPP) Parishad in April 2002, since then no meeting of the Governing Body was held up to February 2005.

6.7. DISTRICT INFORMATION SYSTEM FOR EDUCATION (DISE)

DISE provides extensive data on the school system at the district level and with plans to provide school-based information on education in the entire country in the public domain; this is a wealth of information. If it were complemented with financial data, it would act as a powerful tool to improve the performance of funding towards education as perceived by the common public. The information of public spending on education at the local level and the use of Right to Information by people can create the climate for improving the performance of public funds.

DISE covers all basic tangible and quantitative aspects like infrastructure, human resource, enrolment and results, aids received from the government etc. as we have canvassed in our questionnaire schedule also. But there are some very important intangible (qualitative) factors that are not covered in DISE. We have tried to cover this aspect of the issue also. Information on a child's liking for, involvement with and attention to the activities of the school gives us a larger canvas to work on, in order to judge the efficiency of SSA. We found that these issues are indeed germane. It is hoped that SSA will incorporate such qualitative factors in their information system in future.

6.8. PROCUREMENT PROCEDURE

Procurement plays a vital role in capacity building for implementation of SSA, which assigns great importance to the preparatory activities as these have been conceived as a necessary condition for quality implementation of the programme. Systematic mobilization of the community, creation of an effective decentralized system of decision making, strengthening of the SPO, DPOs and sub-district offices, setting up of an effective information system, assessment of manpower needs are essential for launching and carrying out the programme successfully. These require developing as well as application of an effective procurement system. Procurement covers civil works, equipment, goods, consultancy, resource support etc.

State Project Office did not evolve any specific procurement procedure nor did it provide any guidelines to the subordinate offices in this regard. The infrastructure facilities prevailed in SPO and 10 identified back ward districts under DPEP came as readymade tool under SSA. Need for utilizing fund for development of infrastructure under SSA was reported to have not been felt. The SPO disbursed fund aggregating Rs.133.272 lakh during 2000-01 and 2001-02 to districts not covered by DPEP for pre-project activities. A large portion of this fund related to procurement. The fund was disbursed without undertaking any survey to assess the needs. SPO did not monitor project activities, which required infrastructural development, mobilization of resources, setting up of information system, engagement of professionals (particularly for Management Information System) etc. involving high value procurement on a large scale. No utilization certificates were submitted by the districts nor was there any evidence to show that the SPO called for the same. Entire expenditure was booked in the final head "Project Activities" in accounts.

In respect of interventions where procurement is one of its ingredients, financial requirements relating to procurement were not shown separately in the Budget. There was no analysis to show how the provision was arrived at. In case of procurement/ purchase of specific items like computer, provisions were, however, made in the budget. In Bankura district Rs.15 lakh was provided in the budget for 2004-05 for purhase of computers, but no purchase was made during the financial year. On civil works SSA fund amounting to Rs.19923.769 lakh had been utilized up to December 2004. Bankura District spent Rs.1113.42 lakh upto 2004-05 on that account which mostly related to construction of additional classrooms on centrally prepared estimate as per the norms stipulated in "Frame Work" of SSA. Procurements of materials were made locally and constructions were carried out by engagement of laborers under the supervision of VEC/ WC.

As the accounting personnel engaged on contract basis did not have the expertise to prepare the annual accounts and balance sheet, the same was got done by firm of Chartered Accountants. No record could be produced to the Study Team by the SPO as to the method adopted to select the firm.

6.9. APPOINTMENT OF AUDITOR

Auditing of the accounts of SSA vis-à-vis procedure of selection of Auditor (Chartered Accountant Firm) have been laid down in Chapter-VIII of the Manual. In terms of para 101.7 ibid the selected CA Firm shall be engaged initially for a period of one year. If found suitable, the services of the CA firm may be extended on an annual basis for a maximum of a further two years. In no case should a CA firm be entrusted with the external audit responsibility for a period exceeding three years. But it was observed that

M/s C. Goswami and Co. was appointed as auditor for all DPEP districts and State Office since inception in 1995 and is being continued. After launching of SSA in the State in 2000-01 the same firm was deployed as auditor for SSA accounts also and is continuing the work even upto 2004-05 accounts in violation of clear instructions embodied in the Manual. Papers/ documents regarding appointment and evaluation of the performance of the auditor were not produced to the Team.

It was observed that no procurement plan had been worked out and no set up had been established at any level to assess bulk requirement for the State as well as the districts to handle the same. No delegation of financial powers for procurement to districts/ block level had been made indicating limits, items etc. No terms and conditions were formulated for engagement of external agency in interventions like training, capacity building activities. Rabindra Mukta Vidyalaya was engaged for conduct of bridge course under SSA, while Board of Secondary Education was associated with preparation of various training modules for teachers and village level committee. Total fund spent so far on these accounts was Rs.120.37 lakh. On what terms their services were procured could not be examined as relevant papers/ documents were not made available to the Team by the SPO.

APPENDIX: LIST OF SCHOOLS SURVEYED

No.	Name of the School	Location
1.	Adi Mahakali Pathsala	Bidhan Sarani
2.	Ahiritola Banga Vidyalaya	Ahiritola
3.	Beleghata Deshbandhu Vidyapith	Beleghata
4.	Kishore Bidyapith	Beleghata
5.	Oriental Seminary	Rabindra Sarani
6.	Purba Kolkata Vidyatan	Beleghata
7.	Santi Sangha Siksha Mandir	Behala
8.	Siksha Niketan Vidyalaya for Girls	E.S.I Hospital, Ultadanga
9.	Kankurgachi Vivekananda Vidyapith	Kankurgachi

REFERENCES

'Annual Status of Education Report (Rural) 2006', ASER 2006.
"Sarva Shiksha Abhiyan: A program for elementary education in India" pdf, <http://ssa.nic.in.>
A research report on Out of school children, published by Ministry of Human Resource Development, Department of School Education and Literacy: http://ssa.nic.in/research/Report_ Part_2.pdf
http://nac.nic.in/concept%20papers/ssa.pdf
http://ssa.nic.in/monitoring/West%20Bengal%20Report.pdf
http://ssa.nic.in/statesoc/List%20of%20SPDs.pdf
http://ssa.nic.in/submission/Overview%20on%20Community%20Mobilisation.pdf
http://www.education.nic.in/ssa/ssa_1.asp
http://www.pria.org/panchayat/pdf/SSA_and_Funds.pdf
Report on "Ministry of Human Resource Development, Department of Elementary Education and Literacy, Performance audit report on 'Sarva Shiksha Abhiyan'", 2005-06.
ssa.nic.in/planning/Capacity_Building_4th_JRM_NIAR.pdf
ssa.nic.in/research/Research%20Studies%20Under%20SSA%20for%20website.pdf

INDEX

A

accounting, 23, 50
adaptation, 48
agencies, 13, 15, 22
architecture, 40
assessment, 6, 33, 49
authorities, 10, 36, 37, 38, 41, 42, 43, 48
autonomy, 47

B

balance sheet, 50
base year, 12
budget allocation, 14, 15, 16
buildings, 5, 6, 21

C

Cabinet, 4
capacity building, 24, 49, 51
childhood, 4, 5, 7
class, 18, 27, 29, 31, 32, 33, 39, 40, 41, 42, 43
classroom, 22, 24, 27, 29, 41
climate, 49
community, 4, 5, 6, 7, 10, 21, 22, 28, 49
competition, 35
computer education, 5, 7
conference, 3
convergence, 8
cost, 5, 6, 13, 16, 21, 23

D

data gathering, 25
database, 25
decentralization, 47
deficiencies, 23
delegation, 51
distance education, 22
District Information System for Education (DISE), 49
domestic resources, 14
drinking water, 36, 42

E

economic growth, vii, 1
educational process, 48
electricity, 28
electronic transfer system, 17
elementary school, 4, 28
equality, 46
equipment, 5, 49
equity, 1, 26, 46
European Commission, 13, 17

experiences, 3
expertise, 50

F

feelings, 32
flexibility, 46
flora, 34
flora and fauna, 34
formula, 46
funding, 13, 14, 15, 24, 26, 46, 48, 49

G

gender gap, 4
geography, 34
goal setting, 24
grass, 4, 10, 45
guidelines, 13, 47, 48, 49

H

high school, 22
human resource development, 27

I

illiteracy, 27
India, i, iii, 1, 3, 12, 14, 16, 17, 28, 53
infant mortality, vii, 1
infrastructure, 23, 25, 28, 32, 35, 37, 41, 42, 49
interface, 35
International Development Association (IDA), 13
intervention, 13, 23

K

Kolkata, 1, 32, 39, 40, 41, 43, 51

L

leaks, 27
learning, 3, 5, 24, 42, 48
life expectancy, vii, 1
literacy, 28
local authorities, 48
local community, 48

M

management, 4, 6, 13, 23, 46
management committee, 4, 6
manpower, 49
marriage, 42
minorities, 26
missions, 3
mobile phone, 18
modules, 48, 51
monitoring, 1, 6, 9, 11, 14, 18, 21, 33, 37, 46, 48, 53

N

needy, 37, 40
NGOs, 10, 25, 38

O

offenders, 28
ownership, 10

P

Parliament, 16, 27
poetry, 29
political parties, 27
primary data, 1, 45
primary school, 4, 5, 6, 18, 19, 22, 23, 25, 28, 34, 42

Index

private schools, 21
probe, 31
procurement, 49, 50, 51
programming, 47
project, 1, 7, 31, 41, 42, 50
public domain, 49
purification, 36

Q

Questionnaire, 31

R

radius, 19
reading, 24, 29
real terms, 12
recommendations, v
reliability, 25, 38
repair, 5, 6, 13, 18
replacement, 6
resources, 12, 48, 50
revenue, 22
rewards, 43

S

Sarva Shiksha Abhiyan, i, iii, v, vi, 1, 3, 7, 8, 12, 18, 27, 46, 53
school authority, 33, 41
schooling, 4, 6, 7, 32
screening, 48
secondary data, 1
secondary schools, 28, 42
secondary students, 31, 37
shape, 13
shortage, 19
social category, 4

soft loan, 13
statistics, 28
stereotypes, 28
Student, 40
subsidy, 21
supervision, 1, 8, 10, 50
survey, 1, 19, 22, 31, 32, 40, 50

T

Teacher, 5, 6, 39, 40
teacher training, 22, 48
Teaching aids, 32
textbooks, 5, 6, 21
thoughts, 31
threshold level, 14
training, 4, 5, 6, 22, 23, 48, 51
training programs, 48
transition rate, 25
transportation, 13

U

UK, 13
uniform, 16
urban area, 22

V

vacancies, 23

W

weakness, 48
wealth, 49
World Bank, 13, 17